# Lorita's Adventure

by Magali Jaramillo
Illustrated by Freddie Levin

PEARSON
Scott Foresman

Editorial Offices: Glenview, Illinois • Parsippany, New Jersey • New York, New York
Sales Offices: Needham, Massachusetts • Duluth, Georgia • Glenview, Illinois
Coppell, Texas • Sacramento, California • Mesa, Arizona

"That parrot will never talk," said Edwin. "You've been talking to her for a month. You say, 'Hello Lorita, pretty Lorita.' All that bird does is squawk."

"Be quiet, Edwin," said Flor. "She will talk. It takes a lot of time. Lorita is a smart bird. She'll be talking soon. You'll see!"

Flor got up. She put seeds in Lorita's food dish. She put water in her water dish. "Pretty Lorita," said Flor.

---

**parrot:** tropical bird that sometimes can learn to talk and even sing

**squawk:** make a harsh screaming sound

　　Edwin and Flor went to school. Lorita sat in her cage. She looked out the window. There were green trees. There were colorful flowers. A bird sang, "Chirp, chirp, chirp." Lorita wanted to see everything. She wanted to get out of her cage.

　　Lorita looked at the door of her cage. It wasn't closed all the way! Lorita used her beak. She pushed the door open. Soon she was out of her cage. She flew to the open window. She looked at the trees, flowers, and sky. Then she disappeared out the window.

Lorita flew to the house next door. She landed on the birdbath. "Meow!" she heard. Lorita looked down. There was a cat. Lorita had never seen a cat before.

The cat's name was Mittens. Mittens said, "Meow! Meow! Meow!"

Lorita wanted to talk to Mittens. She didn't know how, but she would try. "Mew. Mew. Meow!" she said.

"Meow!" answered Mittens. She was surprised. A bird that could talk like a cat!

"What are you doing here?" asked Mittens.

"I'm on a journey," said Lorita. "I want to see everything. Meow, meow."

Lorita flew away.

In the next yard, Lorita saw a shady bush. She flew down to get out of the sun. Rocky, the dog, was sleeping under the bush. Lorita had never seen a dog before. *This must be a big cat*, she thought. "Meow, meow!" she said.

Rocky opened his eyes. "Woof," said Rocky. "Woof, woof!"

Lorita wanted to talk to Rocky. "Woo. Woo. Woof!" she said.

Rocky was surprised. This bird could talk like a dog! "What are you doing here?" asked Rocky.

"I'm on a journey," said Lorita. "I want to see everything. Woof, woof."

Lorita flew away.

Lorita heard a beautiful sound. It was a song. Mrs. Taylor was singing as she worked in her garden. Lorita wanted to hear more. She flew down. She landed on Mrs. Taylor's rosebush. Mrs. Taylor didn't notice. She was too busy working and singing.

"It's a lot of fun," she sang, "to work in the sun."

Lorita listened to Mrs. Taylor sing. Lorita wanted to sing too. "La, la, la, la, la," she tried. Then she began to sing, "It's a lot of fun," she sang, "to work in the sun."

Mrs. Taylor looked up. She was surprised. Someone was singing. Where was that singing coming from?

Lorita could meow like a cat. She could woof like a dog. She could sing like Mrs. Taylor. It was time to continue her journey.

---

**continue:** keep going

Lorita was tired. She wanted to go home, but she didn't know the way. How could she find her way home?

Lorita heard a whistle. She knew that whistle. Mr. Li, the mail carrier, whistles like that when he drops off the mail each day. If Lorita followed Mr. Li, maybe she could find her way home.

Lorita flew to Mr. Li. She landed on his mail bag. "I know you," said Mr. Li. "We'll be at your house soon."

Mr. Li whistled as he walked. Lorita whistled too.

When Flor and Edwin came home from school, they made a terrible discovery. Lorita had disappeared. She had opened the door of the cage and had flown away.

"What will we do, Edwin?" cried Flor. "My little Lorita is gone!"

Just then there was a knock at the door. Mr. Li was at the door. Lorita was with him.

"I have a special delivery for you," said Mr. Li with a smile. Lorita hopped off his bag. She hopped on Flor's arm. Soon she was safely back in her cage.

"I'm glad Lorita came back," said Edwin, "even if she can't talk."

"Be quiet, Edwin," said Flor. "Lorita will talk. You'll see!"

"Woof, woof," said Lorita.

Flor and Edwin were surprised. Lorita could woof like Rocky!

"Meow, meow," said Lorita.

Flor and Edwin were even more surprised. Lorita could meow like Mittens!

"See, Edwin," said Flor. "Lorita can meow and woof."

"I hear it, but I don't believe it," said Edwin.

Lorita began to whistle just like Mr. Li. "Listen," said Flor. "Lorita can whistle just like Mr. Li. She is a smart bird."

"I hear it, but I don't believe it!" said Edwin.

"It's a lot of fun," sang Lorita, "to work in the sun."

"Did you hear that, Edwin?" said Flor. "Lorita can sing just like Mrs. Taylor!"

"I hear it, but I don't believe it!" said Edwin.

"It's true," said Flor. "Lorita can meow and woof. She can sing and whistle."

"I still can't believe it," said Edwin, "I thought that parrot could only squawk!"

Lorita looked at Edwin. "Be quiet, Edwin!" she said loudly.

Flor and Edwin laughed and laughed.